You Matter

DANCES OF LIFE

SHARDA STEVENS

ISBN: 9780578969589
Library of Congress: 2021916277
First Printing 2021

Your Journey

One thing I know for sure is, everyone is on a journey. Even if you feel that I have nothing going on in my life, you are still on a journey. The big question is… Where am I going? We are all given the free will to do something great or to not do anything at all. It's all a choice. Now you can read this and say, "Well, you don't know my struggles and what I have been through".

That's true. I don't. But you can't tell me that you do not have the ability to at least try! Try do something that makes this thing called life. Your journey. Worthwhile.

You Matter

Decisions

Starting and stopping has been the name of the game for this past year. Struggling between making money for my family and doing what I love has been the hardest decision. I know people will say don't sleep and grind. Do both! Mentally I could not even imagine not being able to present for daughter, or time for friends, and travel. Maybe that's the sacrifice.

When does your desire to be happy outweigh the money, you need to make to live…? I guess sometimes you must jump! That's what we call faith.

You Matter

Damaged Goods

You know when life hits, the things that you enjoy are put on the bottom of your priority list. However, I just listened to a sermon called "damaged goods" and I said to myself, out loud… Here we go again?!" you are more than a conqueror, "you are the head not the tail", you know what I mean all the same things that you hear when someone is trying to encourage someone. Now please do not get me wrong those religious saying is indeed in the Bible and they are beautiful reminders but sometimes you want to know how you can deal with your issue(s) and what are the steps for those strongholds to be broken. So, to spare you of all the thoughts that ran through my head while watching this sermon. I began to write down all the things that I have been through and the areas in my life that I feel are less than desirable. This allowed me to see what can really hold me back from my potential. I laughed at my list. I literally said OK, so… life has been hard, but you are not the only one. Someone who has been molested, misused, or even lost someone to a tragic death can live again! Here's my suggestion. if you are reading this and you have felt as if your life is mediocre and you have dreams that you want to pursue but you are unsure why you can't take that step. Write those things down. Be honest and ask the Lord how those can "damaged" areas/things in your life can be used for good.

Write that book! Lose those 10lbs! Start that new company!

You Matter

You Matter

The Heart

It always seems like your heart wins. No matter the reason, your heart will say go and you will follow it. Even when it lets you down you still give it a chance to lead you astray all over again. It can also blind what's ugly and put a beautiful perspective in your vision. Your heart can fly you up to cloud 9 and make you cry happy tears. It can love and hate, it can hurt and feel joy.

However if you base your offense according to the Word you can understand why its the bait of the enemy. Bring your offenses to the Lord first, pray, and then talk to the person that offended you. It could be all a misunderstanding or the offense may be intentional. Most often the forgiveness if you and not for them. The recipe for peace is to pray and forgive them.

You Matter

Perform

Sometimes I think that we rather have someone in our lives that says they loves us versus us being someone who shows that action. Go ahead… ask yourself are you truly loved and happy or do you keep them around because they SAY those 3 magic words? We all long for companionship however what is the cost? What do you sacrifice?

Self-love can be hard but it's necessary. When you love yourself, you will see how beautiful that translate is all aspects of your life.

YOU MATTER

Triggers

I know the saying "forgive but don't forget" is popular however the forgetting is what I wish could happen. Something as small as a sound or smell can trigger a happy, angry, or sad memory/moment. Sometimes you can feel all those emotions at the same time.

If it triggers? Does it mean that you have not forgiven or that you are not completely healed? One thing I know is that it should be expressed, not in a dangerous way but to help you heal. Dancing, therapy, expressive writing etc. Don't be ashamed if something makes you feel a way. Be self-aware. Love who and where you are in every aspect of your life. IT'A OK TO BE HUMAN

You Matter

Purpose

Your purpose is normally something you are already doing however distractions, laziness, and procrastination can make you feel like there is no purpose in sight. Something as simple as what makes you happy or feel accomplished is sometimes the calling that God has on your life. Your purpose can make you scared, can make you feel inadequate, or the very thing that makes you feel alive can scare you.

Sidenote: remember when you are stepping into your purpose don't allow comparison to get in the way! It will surely kill your joy. Whatever someone else is doing, cheer them on but don't stare too long because You Matter too.

USED

Being used is inevitable we all have been used or used others in some type of capacity. Often, I allow myself to be used, to keep pouring until I have nothing left. I go back to when I was a child and heard my mom say" treat those how you would like to be treated "and that has stuck with me.

I wait for those to deposit what they have withdrew and it never amounts to the exact change. I perform for their love and wait for them to cheer. I dive into the deep end and doggy paddle for as long as I can and wait to be saved. I juggle so many glass balls and wait for someone to say, "hey I am open throw me a ball". So that's where boundaries must be in place. Sometimes who must love people from a far, say no to engagements, and be a little more selfish. Even when your inner core is to love deeply and give often. Reciprocation must happen so your love tank can be fueled.

Remember YOU Matter